SCHIRMER
PERFORMANCE
EDITIONS

# BAROQUE TO MODERN

## Upper Intermediate Level

21 Pieces by 18 Composers in Progressive Order

Compiled and Edited by Richard Walters

*On the cover:*
Detail from *Trompe l'oeil. Board Partition
with Letter Rack and Music Book* (1668)
by Cornelius Norbertus Gysbrechts (c. 1630–1675)

Detail from *Colored Composition of Forms* (1914)
by August Macke (1887–1914)

ISBN 978-1-4950-8863-6

# G. SCHIRMER, *Inc.*

DISTRIBUTED BY

HAL•LEONARD®

www.halleonard.com

Contact us:
**Hal Leonard**
7777 West Bluemound Road
Milwaukee, WI 53213
Email: info@halleonard.com

In Europe, contact:
**Hal Leonard Europe Limited**
42 Wigmore Street
Marylebone, London, W1U 2RN
Email: info@halleonardeurope.com

In Australia, contact:
**Hal Leonard Australia Pty. Ltd.**
4 Lentara Court
Cheltenham, Victoria, 3192 Australia
Email: info@halleonard.com.au

# CONTENTS

Though the table of contents appears in alphabetical order
by composer, the music in this book is in progressive order.

# COMPOSER BIOGRAPHIES, HISTORICAL NOTES

## AND

# PRACTICE AND PERFORMANCE TIPS

## JOHANN SEBASTIAN BACH
(1685–1750, German)

One of the greatest composers in the history of music, J. S. Bach defined the high Baroque style, developing counterpoint in composition further than any composer before him or since. However, during his lifetime he was more known for his virtuoso organ and harpsichord playing than for composition. Relatively few people were familiar with the works of J.S. Bach in the decades after his death. The modern wide recognition of Bach as a master composer began in the mid-nineteenth century, decades after his death, first championed by Felix Mendelssohn. Throughout his life Bach wrote keyboard music for his students, including his children. Bach composed hundreds of works, most for practical occasions, including cantatas, oratorios, motets, various instrumental suites, harpsichord works, organ works, and orchestral pieces. He came from a long line of musicians, and was father to six noted composers.

### Invention No. 8 in F Major, BWV 779
*Practice and Performance Tips*
- Bach gave us no tempo, but this happy piece should be played *allegro*.
- Play all eighth notes slightly detached.
- Begin practice slowly, hands separately, building to slow practice, hands together.
- Strive for absolute evenness and steadiness of tempo.
- Practicing scales as you practice this invention will help.
- Bach gave no dynamics. We don't recommend extreme contrasts in this piece.

### Prelude in D Major, BWV 936
*Practice and Performance Tips*
- Bach gave no tempo indication or dynamics. Editorial suggestions appear in brackets. There are other options regarding dynamics.
- The trill begins on the note above.
- Aim for steadiness and evenness throughout.
- Start with slow practice, hands separately, building to slow practice, hands together.
- Play the left-hand eighth notes slightly detached.
- There should be a good-natured sense of contentment in a good performance.

## SAMUEL BARBER
(1910–1981, American)

Born in Pennsylvania, Samuel Barber was a precocious musical talent who composed from an early age, and at fourteen began studies in singing, piano, and composition at the Curtis Institute. One of the most prominent American composers of the twentieth century, he is remembered for his distinctive neo-Romantic style. Early in his career he performed as a singer, which may have helped him develop an aptitude for writing the lyrical melodies that define his works. Barber wrote for orchestra, voice, choir, piano, chamber ensemble, and solo instruments and was acclaimed during his lifetime. After 1938, almost all of his compositions were written on commission from renowned performers and ensembles. Among his well-known pieces are the *Adagio for Strings* (1936), the opera *Vanessa* (1956–57), *Knoxville: Summer of 1915* (1947), and *Hermit Songs* (1953).

## Poison Ivy
### from *Fresh from West Chester (Some Jazzings)*

"Poison Ivy" is from a two-piece set, *Fresh from West Chester (Some Jazzings)*, composed at age fifteen in 1925. The teenage Barber attempts some humor in the comments in the score. This was unpublished until 2010.

*Practice and Performance Tips*
- Play the quarter-note chords in the right hand with slight separation.
- The tempo should stay steady and insistent, played with crisp rhythm.
- Use no sustaining pedal except in measures 25–34.
- The most challenging spot in the piece is the left hand of measures 21–24. Practice this separately to work up to the speed and accuracy needed.
- Your final tempo should be determined by how fast you can gracefully play the left hand in measures 21–24.
- Barber's indication of "sock it" in measure 25 indicates to play measures 25–28 assertively, with rigorous rhythm, spirit and volume. Keep this in tempo; do not slow down.
- Barber's comment "with itching" in measure 35 indicates that the right hand should not be played *legato*.
- "Bad memories" in measure 45 is the teenage Barber's attempt at a joke; the music is a recapitulation of the music of the opening section.

## BÉLA BARTÓK
(1881–1945, Hungarian;
became a US citizen in 1945)

Béla Bartók is one of the most important and often performed composers of the twentieth century, and much of his music, including *Concerto for Orchestra*, his concertos, his string quartets, and his opera *Bluebeard's Castle*, holds a venerable position in the classical repertoire. His parents were amateur musicians who nurtured their young son with exposure to dance music, drumming, and piano lessons. In 1899 he started piano and composition studies at the Academy of Music in Budapest. Not long after graduation, he joined the Academy's piano faculty. Bartók wished to create music that was truly Hungarian at its core, a desire that sparked his deep interest in folk music. His work collecting and studying folksongs from around the Baltic region impacted his own compositional style greatly in terms of rhythm, mood, and texture. Bartók utilized folk influences to create a truly unique style. Though

he composed operas, concertos, ballets, and chamber music, he was also committed to music education and composed several piano works for students, including his method *Mikrokosmos*. Bartók toured extensively in the 1920s and '30s, and became well-known as both a pianist and composer. He immigrated to the US in 1940 to escape war and political turmoil in Europe, and settled in New York City. The last years of his life were difficult with many health problems.

## Joc cu bâta (Stick Dance)
### from *Roumanian Folk Dances*

The set of *Roumanian Folk Dances* was composed in 1915, later transcribed for violin and piano.

*Practice and Performance Tips*
- Practice the right hand alone, incorporating the articulation and dynamics from the beginning. Play the right hand alone over and over to obtain a strong sense of the melody.
- Practice the left hand alone, incorporating the articulation and dynamics, and especially the very specific pedaling that Bartók has composed.
- Practice slowly hands together, retaining all the details of articulation and dynamics, and keeping a steady tempo.
- The performance should be insistently steady in tempo, with a lively, dancelike sense of rhythm.
- Do not over pedal! Lower the sustaining pedal only at the exact point Bartók has indicated, and release exactly so as well.

## LUDWIG VAN BEETHOVEN
(1770–1827, German)

Beethoven was the major figure of the transition from the Classical Era to the Romantic Era in music. As one of the first successful freelance composers, as opposed to a composer thriving in a royal court appointment, Beethoven wrote widely in nearly every genre of his day, with emphasis on instrumental music. He acquired wealth and fame beyond any composer before him. Beethoven's chamber music, piano sonatas, concertos, and symphonies are part of the ever present international repertoire. In his youth he was regarded as one of the greatest pianists of his time, but he stopped performing after hearing loss set in. He devoted an enormous amount of his compositional efforts to the piano, which as an instrument came of age during his lifetime. He was occasionally a piano teacher, with wealthy patrons and young prodigies begging for lessons, though this task was not a match for his nature. However, teaching piano did inspire him to write many pieces for students. Because his piano music is so widely spread across the level of difficulty from easy to virtuosic, Beethoven's piano music is played by students and professional pianists.

### Bagatelle in A minor ("Für Elise"), WoO 59

Bagatelle in A minor ("Für Elise"), WoO 59 was composed between 1808 and 1810, but was unpublished until 1867. It was originally titled "Für Therese," and was written for the young woman to whom Beethoven proposed marriage. She refused him. The original publisher misread Beethoven's scratchy handwriting, and it's been "Für Elise" ever since.

*Practice and Performance Tips*
- Beethoven's tempo of *poco moto* (a little motion) could be widely interpreted. However, do not take it too fast. Something around eighth note = 120 perhaps.
- Practice in sections. Section 1: measures 1–23; section 2: measures 24–38; section 3: measures 39–60; section 4: measures 61-83; section 5: measures 84–105.
- The recurring music (measures 1–23) should be played ultimately quietly, flowing. However, early stages of practice it may help to play *mf* until secure in the notes.
- Some slurring has been suggested (in brackets), as well as pedaling.
- Keep a steady tempo when you play the thirty second notes in measures 32–36. The speed at which you can play this section is your performance tempo.
- Make sure the left-hand repeated notes in measures 61–76 are played evenly, and not too heavily.
- Take special care in practicing the right hand in measures 79–84.

## FRÉDÉRIC CHOPIN
(1810–1849, Polish/French)

A major Romantic era composer for piano, Chopin created a uniquely personal, forward-thinking style, and revolutionized literature for the instrument. He left his native Poland at age 20 after an education at the Warsaw Conservatory, first briefly to Vienna before settling in Paris for most of the remainder of his life. Chopin became a much sought after piano teacher in the French capital, and was part of the lively salon culture, where he preferred to perform instead of in large concert halls. He is reputed to have had an extremely refined, poetic touch as a pianist. He was in chronic frail health through much of his adult life, and died at the young age of 39, probably brought on by tuberculosis. Because of political upheaval, Chopin was never able to return to Poland, and his nostalgic ache for his homeland is a characteristic heard in his music.

### Prelude in D-flat Major ("Raindrop"), Op. 28, No. 15

*Practice and Performance Tips*
- When learning music from the romantic era, it helps to approach it very dryly at first, just getting the notes and rhythms secure. This is done with slow practice and without pedal.
- The flights of melody in measures 4, 23 and 79 need to be played quite gracefully but fleet. Practice these spots with great care. They should not sound forceful.
- Play the grace notes before the beat.
- The editor of this edition of the prelude, Brian Ganz states about measure 2: "I have followed closely the notation of Chopin's manuscript of this prelude. Note Chopin's consistent notation in this and similar measures: the C is a dotted half note; the E-flat and G-flat are half notes. However, I do not believe it is necessary to make excessive efforts to release the E-flat and G-flat precisely at the third beat. Rather, I believe Chopin is implying a "finger pedal" for added sonorous richness. In any case, Chopin's pedal markings clearly extend the E-flat and G-flat beyond the notated values. (Note that use of finger pedal may be concurrent with use of the foot pedal.) On the other hand, I do urge the performer to adhere strictly to the holding of voices as notated, as with the leading tone (i.e., middle C) in measures 3 and 4. Such examples of tonal fullness through the use of finger pedal help to offset the monotony threatened by the repetition of the A-flat, or fifth degree of the tonic chord. Carefully note all examples of finger pedal in this prelude, e.g. the extra-stemmed A-flat in measures 3, 7 and elsewhere, and the extra-stemmed G-flat of measure 19."
- Maintain *p* until measure 28, then a very slowly paced *crescendo* begins in the left hand. The right hand joins in the *crescendo* in measure 35. Carefully pacing the *crescendo* until the arrival at *ff* in measure 40 is the musical challenge.
- The *subito p* in measure 43 begins another long *crescendo* to *ff* in measure 56 that needs to be carefully paced.
- There are particulars to Brian Ganz's edition of this prelude. To read more visit this website: www.halleonard.com/item_detail.jsp?itemid=296523

## CLAUDE DEBUSSY
(1862–1918, French)

One of the greatest French composers in history, Debussy created a distinct style of music that set itself apart from the Romantic era aesthetics. Born in the western suburbs of Paris to working class parents, he began piano lessons and soon, at the age of ten, was accepted into classes in piano and theory at the Paris Conservatoire. Young Claude dreamed of becoming a concert pianist, but started composition study at age eighteen, and by 1883 had won major prizes for his cantata *L'enfant prodigue*. He is a revered for a large body of work, including operas, ballets, orchestral music, choral music, chamber works, songs, and quite a lot of piano music. He also was editor for a Durand edition of Chopin's piano music. Debussy's colorful harmonic style is sometimes called impressionism, a term borrowed from the label given French painters of the 1870s and 1880s, such as Claude Monet.

### La fille aux cheveux de lin
### from *Préludes*, Book 1, L. 117, No. 8
"La fille qux cheveux de lin" (The girl with the flaxen hair) comes from the first book of *Préludes*, which were composed in 1912–13.

*Practice and Performance Tips*
- The top notes of the right hand are the melody, and should be slightly brought out.
- Begin early practice at a slightly louder dynamic than $p$, to become secure in the music
- Try to achieve as much *legato* as possible using the fingers only, without the sustaining pedal.
- Have the discipline to practice without sustaining pedal. Only when you have learned the piece well should you begin to add pedal
- The most common mistake in playing Debussy is too much pedal. Keep the harmonies clear.
- Some spots require extra practice for most, including measures 24–27 and measure 35.
- In the third beat of measure 6 in the left hand, play the low E-flat and B-flat as sort of grace note before the beat, then the hand jumps up to play the higher G and B-flat.
- Debussy used the parallel slashes at the end of measure 11 to simply say that the "cédez" (a slowing of the tempo) ends. He did not intend a lifting of the hands. The same is true of measures 23 and 27.
- The climax is only *mf*. Keep it contained.

## NORMAN DELLO JOIO
(1913–2008, American)

One of the most notable American composers in mid-20th century, Norman Dello Joio grew up in a musical home in New York City, the son of an Italian immigrant father who worked as an organist, pianist, singer, and vocal coach. Musicians were constantly in the home, including singers from the Metropolitan Opera who came for coaching sessions. Norman took organ lessons from his godfather, Pietro Yon (composer of the Christmas classic "Gesù Bambino"), a composer and the organist for St. Patrick's Cathedral in New York. Dello Joio worked as an organist in his teens, before deciding to turn his attention to composition instead. After initial composition study at the Institute of Musical Art and the Juilliard School, he began studying with Paul Hindemith at the Yale School of Music. Hindemith encouraged Dello Joio to embrace the natural tonal lyricism of his writing (as opposed to the atonality then in vogue), which was infused with the spirit of Italian opera and the church music of his childhood, as well as early jazz. Dello Joio remained true to his style in writing operas, ballets, orchestra pieces, solo instrumental works, art songs, piano music, and choral music. He was on the faculties of Sarah Lawrence College, the Mannes College of Music, and Boston University. In 1957, the Young Composers Project, which placed composers under the age of thirty-five as composers-in-residence of public high schools around the country, was founded based upon Dello Joio's suggestion.

### Bright from *Suite for Piano*
"Bright" is the second of four movements from *Suite for Piano*, composed in 1940.

*Practice and Performance Tips*
- This piece may not work for someone who cannot reach a minor 10th in the left hand (measure 3 and elsewhere), because at this tempo and in this style it is not possible to roll this chord.
- Learn the articulations (slurs, *staccatos*, *staccato* with *tenuto* markings, etc.) from the beginning as you learn the notes, as the articulations are such an integral part of the rhythmic structure of the composition.
- Practice hands separately, without pedal.
- The piece is best played without sustaining pedal. However, pedal could be added to very specific spots. Example: beat 1 (only) of measure 15 to connect the slur.

- The style changes to quasi-*legato* in measure 23.
- Steadiness and rhythm are paramount in performance, as well as the crisp observance of all dynamics and articulations.
- One might choose to play beat 2 of measure 36 entirely in the right hand, leaving the left hand ready for the low note that follows.

## EDVARD GRIEG
(1843–1907, Norwegian)

Grieg was the great Norwegian composer of the nineteenth century. After childhood in Bergen in a richly musical family he entered the Leipzig Conservatory at age 15, where he was exposed to the major German musicians and composers of the day. He returned to Norway at age 19, and soon became acquainted with Norwegian folk music, which would be the source of inspiration for his individual musical style. Recognition as a composer and pianist led to Grieg's appointment as conductor of the Philharmonic Society in Oslo; he also founded the Norwegian Academy of Music. Through travel and musical connections he became a part of the international music scene of his day, in contact with many major musical figures. Grieg was an excellent pianist, and his piano music shows an idiomatic understanding of the instrument.

### Nottorno from *Lyric Pieces*, Op. 54, No. 4
The *Lyric Pieces* are short character works composed in nine sets from 1867 to 1901. Op. 54 was composed in 1891.

*Practice and Performance Tips*
- Don't make the mistake of trying to sensitively play a lovely, romantic piece such as this from the beginning of practice. Have the discipline to break the music down and learn it thoroughly and cleanly before applying full expression to it.
- Also, have the discipline to practice without the sustaining pedal. The sustaining pedal, is integral to the piece, but practicing without will reveal anything that needs more clarity.
- Through much of the piece there are essentially three musical voices: the treble melody, the bass line, and the inner voice, such as the repeated chords in measures 1–20.
- Keep the repeated chords quiet.
- The grace notes should be gently played before the beat throughout.
- The section that begins in measure 21 is probably best practiced slowly, hands together.
- Measure 33 may be extended a bit as the sound disappears to nothing (*al niente*).

- Do not rush through the grace note arpeggio in the final measure.

## DMITRI KABALEVSKY
(1904–1987, Russian)

Kabalevsky was an important Russian composer of the Soviet era who wrote music in many genres, including four symphonies, a handful of operas, theatre and film scores, patriotic music, choral music, vocal music, and numerous piano works. He embraced the Soviet notion of socialist realism in art, a fact that was politically advantageous to his career in the USSR. While studying piano and composition at the Moscow Conservatory, he taught piano lessons at a music college and it was for these students that he began writing works for young players. In 1932 he started teaching at the Moscow Conservatory, earning the title of professor in 1939. He eventually went on to develop programs for the concert hall, radio, and television aimed at teaching children about classical music. In the last decades of his life, Kabalevsky focused on developing music curricula for schools, retiring from the Moscow Conservatory to teach in public schools where he could test his theories and the effectiveness of his syllabi. This he considered his true life's work, and his pedagogical principles revolutionized music education in Russia. A collection of his writings on music education was published in English in 1988 as *Music and Education: A Composer Writes About Musical Education*.

### Selections from 30 Pieces for Children, Op. 27
Kabalevsky often quoted Maxim Gorki, saying that books for children should be "the same as for adults, only better." Kabalevsky believed strongly in writing music for young players that was not dumbed-down, but rather, complete, imaginative compositions unto themselves. This was composed in 1937–38. Kabalevsky did a slight revision of Op. 27 in 1985, which was intended to be an authoritative edition. (This is our source for the pieces in this collection.)

### War Dance (No. 19)
*Practice and Performance Tips*
- As the title suggests, the piece should be played rhythmically and aggressively and very steadily.
- Practice first at a slow tempo, and increase the tempo as you master the music.
- The slurs, *staccato* markings and accents must be astutely observed for the character of the music to come through.
- Pay attention to which notes receive which kind of accent, and which notes have no accents.

- Dynamic contrasts make this music exciting. Observe what the composer has written.
- Emphasize the *subito **p*** in measures 9 and 18.
- Use no sustaining pedal at all except in the spots the composer has indicated.

### Etude in A Major (No. 26)

*Practice and Performance Tips*
- This is a brilliant showpiece that dazzles if well played.
- Notice the melody that in general is shown with the *tenuto* stress markings; bring this out.
- Practice hands separately and slowly at first.
- Move to slow practice, hands together.
- Increase your tempo as you master the music, but keep it steady whatever the tempo.
- Pay careful attention to the articulation and pedaling that Kabalevsky has composed.
- Practice the pedaling when playing left hand alone.
- Use no sustaining pedal except where indicated.

## ARAM KHACHATURIAN
(1903–1978, Soviet/Armenian)

Aram Khachaturian was a seminal figure in 20th century Armenian and Soviet culture. Beloved in his homeland for bringing Armenia to prominence within the realm of Western art music, a major concert hall in Armenia's capital Yerevan bears his name, as well as a string quartet and an international competition for piano and composition. Born in Tbilisi, Georgia, of Armenian heritage, he grew up listening to Armenian folk songs but was also exposed to classical music early on through the Tbilisi's chapter of the Russian Music Society, the city's Italian Opera Theater, and visits by musicians such as Sergei Rachmaninoff. He moved to Moscow to study composition in 1921. Khachaturian's musical language combined Armenian folk influences with the Russian romantic tradition, embodying the official Soviet arts policy. He used traditional forms, such as theme and variations, sonata form, and Baroque suite forms, in creative ways, juxtaposing them with Armenian melodies and religious songs, folk dance rhythms, and a harmonic language that took inspiration from folk instruments such as the saz. He wrote symphonies, instrumental concertos, sonatas, ballets, and was the first Armenian composer to write film music. Khachaturian's most recognizable composition to the general public is "Sabre Dance" from the ballet *Gayane*. Starting in 1950, he also became active as an internationally touring conductor. He was awarded the Order of Lenin in 1939 and the Hero of Socialist Labor in 1973.

### Etude from *Children's Album,* Book 1
*Children's Album*, Volume 1 was composed in 1947. A Schirmer edition from the 1970s called the set *Adventures of Ivan* and applied titles different from Khachaturian's originals. The piece below was called "Ivan Is Very Busy" in that edition. "Etude" is the original title.

*Practice and Performance Tips*
- It will help to divide the music into sections for practice. Section 1: measures 1–12; section 2: measures 13–21; section 3: measures 22–35; section 4: measures 36–51; section 5: measures 52–63; section 6: measures 64–76.
- Rather than become overwhelmed by practicing the entire piece, practice only one section at a time in early stages.
- Practice hands together and slowly, learning the articulation as you learn the notes.
- It may be easier for some student pianists to first learn the ***p*** or ***pp*** sections at ***mf***, then after mastering the music play at ***p*** or ***pp***.
- Only increase the tempo when you have mastered a section. Always keep a steady beat whatever the tempo.
- Your goal eventually in performance is clarity of all notes and rhythms, crisp observance of all dynamics, a tempo fast enough to conjure the complex busy-ness of the music, and steadiness of tempo in achieving all this.

## FELIX MENDELSSOHN
(1809–1847, German)

One of the most talented musical prodigies in history, Felix grew up in a cultured, upper middle-class home in Berlin. The Mendelssohn family converted from Judaism to Christianity when Felix was seven years old, and the family name was changed to Mendelssohn-Bartholdy. As a boy he excelled in drawing and poetry, as well as in music. His biggest influences were Bach and Mozart, thus he had more of a Classical temperament than the Romantic one of his era. Mendelssohn created an enormous body of work in his short life, including operas, concertos, symphonies, chamber music, songs, organ works, choral music and, of course, piano music. He was one of the major figures in German music of the nineteenth century, not only as a composer, but also as a conductor and traveled widely. He founded the Leipzig Conservatory in 1843 It was Mendelssohn who led the revival of J.S. Bach's music, which had been forgotten by then by most. Mendelssohn died from a series of strokes at the young age of 38.

### Song Without Words in F-sharp minor ("Venetian Gondola Song") from *Songs Without Words*, Op. 30, No. 6

His second book of *Songs Without Words* (Lieder ohne Worte) was composed in 1833–34. This is the sixth and last of the set.

*Practice and Performance Tips*
- Give the left-hand accompaniment figure lots of attention in practice. This should, over time, achieve fluency and ease.
- Notice that Mendelssohn marked the left hand *p* and the right hand *f* in measure 3, requiring independence of hands in dynamics.
- Practice the right-hand melody alone, aiming for a graceful singing quality.
- It will take quite a bit of practice for most before you can achieve the tranquil mood.
- Practice the trill that begins in measure 32 separately, until it's not only soft and fast, but also expressive, with a hairpin at its center.
- The composer has written many dynamics, and each needs attention.

## ROBERT MUCZYNSKI
(1929–2010, American)

Composer and pianist Robert Muczynski studied at DePaul University in his hometown of Chicago with Alexander Tcherepnin. A brilliant pianist, at twenty nine he made his Carnegie Hall debut with a performance of his own compositions. In addition to solo piano works, Muczynski mainly wrote for small chamber ensembles and also composed several orchestral pieces. His flute and saxophone sonatas, as well as *Time Pieces* for clarinet and piano, have become part of the standard repertoire for those instruments. In 1981, his concerto for saxophone was nominated for the Pulitzer Prize. Muczynski was composer in residence on the faculty of the University of Arizona from 1965 until his retirement in 1988.

### Morning Promenade
from *A Summer Journal*, Op. 19, No. 1

*A Summer Journal* was composed in 1964. The set evokes the sounds and moods of summer. The composer stated about deliberately writing for a contained level of difficulty, "Again, I cut myself to the bone, setting out to make as much out of as little as possible."

*Practice and Performance Tips*
- Though this may sound modern to someone unaccustomed to twentieth century music, it is a good example of an approachable work by a composer who was considered conservative in his time. Musical tastes have become more conservative since 1964 regarding dissonance.
- Though angular in its lines, this is essentially a lyrical piece.
- The composer intends a different articulation for those notes not marked with a slur, for instance, all the notes of measure 1.
- Try playing those notes not marked with slurs *portato*, with slight separation, so there is contrast with the *legato* playing of the slurred notes.
- Make the most of the strong dynamic contrasts.
- The trill in measure 13 becomes a single note on beat 1 of measure 14; the trill does not continue until beat 2.
- We suggest no sustaining pedal for section 1 (through measure 27).
- The chordal section that begins in measure 28 has the spirit of a soulful chorale.
- Savor the harmonies in the chords in this section, and move from chord to chord as smoothly as possible, with discriminating use of the sustaining pedal.
- In pedaling the chords, be sure to keep the harmonies very clear, not blurred.

## PIETRO DOMENICO PARADIES
[PARADISI] (1707–1791, Italian)

Paradisi (his original name) spent many unsuccessful years in Italy, attempting to establish himself as an opera composer. Failed stage works in Naples and Venice caused him to seek employment in London, where he changed his name to Paradies, as a teacher and composer of harpsichord music. He later moved back to Italy to retire. Though his vocal works never gained the notoriety he wished, his Twelve Sonatas for Gravicembalo (a predecessor to the piano) became extremely popular during his life and into the next century.

### Toccata from Sonata No. 6 in A Major

The second movement of the sixth sonata is a perennial favorite of student pianists today, often published separately as "Toccata." A toccata is a brilliant composition showing virtuoso playing.

*Practice and Performance Tips*
- The greatest challenge is to master steadiness and evenness in the sixteenth notes from start to finish.
- Any student pianist will need to practice hands alone slowly. The right hand particularly needs much slow practice.

- Because it is a lengthy piece, your practice should be divided into short sections.
- The eighth notes of the left hand, primarily, should be played detached throughout.
- In your practice you should gradually increase your speed as you master the music. Your ultimate tempo can only be as fast as you can manage. Just be sure the tempo you choose is steady and one that sounds controlled and is not running away from you.
- This toccata is not really about dynamic contrasts, and we have not suggested any. This piece will make its impact purely through even playing from start to finish.

## SERGEI PROKOFIEV
(1891–1953, Russian)

Russian composer and pianist Sergei Prokofiev pushed the boundaries of Russian romanticism without fully disregarding its influence. Influenced by the formal aspects of works by Haydn and Mozart, he was also a pioneering neo-classicist. Prokofiev was born in eastern Ukraine, but travelled often with his mother to Moscow and St. Petersburg where he was exposed to works such as Gounod's *Faust*, Borodin's *Prince Igor*, Tchaikovsky's *Sleeping Beauty*, and operas such as *La Traviata* and *Carmen*. His prodigious musical abilities as a child led him to lessons with Reinhold Glière and then studies at the St. Petersburg Conservatory. He composed several sonatas and symphonies during his studies, as well as his first piano concerto, which he played for his piano exam at the conservatory, taking first prize. In 1917, following the October Revolution, he left Russia, first moving to the United States and then settling in Europe. He continued to tour internationally after returning to the Soviet Union in 1936, until the authorities confiscated his passport two years later. During World War II Prokofiev was evacuated from the USSR. It was a difficult time for composers and artists in Soviet Russia. Between 1946 and '48, Soviet political leader Andrey Zhdanov passed a number of resolutions with the intent of heavily regulating artistic output and keeping it in line with the ideals of socialist realism and the Communist Party.

### Selections from *Music for Children*, Op. 65
The twelve pieces in *Music for Children* were composed in 1935, a break from working on the ballet *Romeo and Juliet*.

### Tarantella (No. 4)
*Practice and Performance Tips*
- A Tarantella is a fast folk dance of southern Italy (originally from the town of Taranto). It is characterized as being in 6/8, with shifts from minor to major.
- Begin with slow practice, hands together.
- As a default, play all notes slightly separated, except those marked with a slur (for instance, left hand measure 2 and 6; right hand measure 8, etc.)
- It may help some students to learn the notes and rhythms first at *mf*, then when mastered apply the composer's dynamics.
- Increase the speed when the music feels comfortable under your fingers.
- Listen for steadiness and evenness as you play.
- Playing this music quickly and at a contained dynamic (*mp* or *p*) requires finger finesse.
- Listen for steadiness and evenness as you play.
- Notice the varied melody when the opening material returns in measure 49.
- In setting your final performance tempo, determine how quickly you can play the most difficult spots for you; then play the entire piece at the tempo you can manage in those spots.
- No sustaining pedal is recommended at all, except for possibly the final two measures.

### March of the Grasshoppers (No. 7)
*Practice and Performance Tips*
- Though it is marked *f*, there should be a buoyant, not stiff, tone to the opening.
- Practice hands separately and slowly for the section measures 17–29 before putting the hands together.
- Notice the change of texture at measure 17, to phrased *legato* playing.
- Practice the right-hand melody alone in the section beginning in measure 31, creating phrase as composed.
- Practice left hand alone measures 30–41, mastering the wide leaps.
- Use no sustaining pedal throughout.
- Insightfully realize all the composer's dynamics and articulations, which will bring wit to the performance.

## ROBERT SCHUMANN
(1810–1856, German)

One of the principal composers of the Romantic era, Robert Schumann's relatively short creative career gave the world major repertoire in symphonies, art song, chamber music, and piano music. Besides being a composer, Schumann was an accomplished writer about music, especially as a critic, then editor of the influential *Neue*

*Zeitschrift für Musik*. He was married to concert pianist Clara Wieck, who championed his works after his death, the result a severe struggle with mental illness. Schumann was an early supporter of the young Johannes Brahms.

### Träumerei (Reverie) from *Scenes from Childhood* (*Kinderszenen*), Op. 15, No. 7

Schumann made a specialty of short character pieces for piano, not entirely unrelated to his distinctive work as a major composer of art song. *Scenes from Childhood* (Kinderszenen) is a set of thirteen pieces composed in 1838. The famous "Träumerei" is nostalgic and dreamy.

*Practice and Performance Tips*
- Have the discipline to practice this beautiful music hands alone, making every detail clear and precise.
- Force yourself to practice slowly and without sustaining pedal, so you can hear every detail.
- When pedal is added, listen carefully so that harmony remains clear.
- Don't let the performance tempo be so slow that there is no flow to the melody.
- In measure 6 on beat 2, play both the lower notes in the treble clef with the thumb. The same is true on beat 2 of measure 22.

## DMITRI SHOSTAKOVICH
(1906–1975, Russian)

A major mid-20th century composer, Shostakovich is famous for his epic symphonies, concertos, operas, string quartets, and other chamber works. Born in St. Petersburg, his entire career took place in Soviet-era Russia. His life teetered between receiving high official honors and living with an almost debilitating fear of arrest for works that did not adhere to the Soviet ideals of socialist realism. In 1934, his opera *Lady Macbeth of the Mtsensk District* met with great popular success, but was banned by Stalin for the next thirty years as modernist, surrealist, and obscene. The following year, Stalin began a campaign known as the Purges, executing or exiling to prison camps politicians, intellectuals, and artists. Shostakovich managed to avoid such a fate, and despite an atmosphere of anxiety and repression, was able to compose an astounding number of works with originality, humor, and emotional power. He succeeded in striking a balance between modernism and tradition that continues to make his music accessible to a broad audience. An excellent pianist, Shostakovich performed concertos by Mozart,

Prokofiev, and Tchaikovsky early in his career, but after 1930 limited himself to performing his own works and some chamber music. He taught instrumentation and composition at the Leningrad Conservatory from 1937–1968, with brief breaks due to war and other political disruptions, and at the Moscow Conservatory in the 1940s. Since his death in 1975, Shostakovich has become one of the most-performed 20th century composers.

### Lyrical Waltz from *Dances of the Dolls*

*Dances of the Dolls* is a suite of piano pieces compiled in 1953 by the composer from his Ballet Suites (comprised of excerpts from ballets, incidental music and film scores). "Lyrical Waltz" comes from Ballet Suite No. 2. Shostakovich himself made the piano solo versions for *Dances of the Dolls*.

*Practice and Performance Tips*
- One might mistake this for a traditional Viennese or Parisian waltz for a bit, until Shostakovich's chromaticism emerges.
- This waltz needs effortless grace and elegance.
- The melody needs to be phrased carefully, creating the lyricism of the title.
- Practice the left hand alone to obtain the touch and the pedaling the composer has indicated. In typical waltz style beat 1 is slurred to beat 2, and beat 3 is separated.
- Carefully practice pedaling throughout, using only that which the composer has indicated.
- Playing the slurs and *staccatos* in measures 36–48 will give the music lightness and color.
- Note the quiet ending. You might experiment, going from ***p*** in measure 76 to ***pp*** by the last line.
- A slight *ritardando* is possible going into the final chord.

## TAN DUN
(b. 1957, Chinese)

Chinese-American composer Tan Dun came of age during the Cultural Revolution, a time when education and musical expression were severely repressed. He was born in a rural town in the Hunan Province, a historic area with a dramatic natural landscape and strong attachment to shamanistic culture. He worked planting rice on a commune for several years in his youth, learning traditional Chinese string instruments and collecting folk songs in his free time. When the restriction of the Cultural Revolution finally began to lift and music schools reopened, Tan began studying composition at the Central Conservatory of Music in Beijing.

There he studied music by Bartók, Schoenberg, and Boulez, as well as contemporary composers such as Crumb, Henze, and Takemitsu who visited the conservatory. Tan was considered a leading composer of the Chinese "New Way," a group of artists who dominated artistic life in China in the post-Cultural Revolution era of the 1980s. In 1986 he moved to New York City, entering the doctoral program in composition at Columbia University where he studied with Chou Wen-chung, Mario Davidovsky, and George Edwards. Tan is often commissioned to write pieces by the world's leading ensembles and cultural festivals, including the Metropolitan Opera, the New York Philharmonic, and the Edinburgh Festival. In 2001 he won an Academy Award for best music score for the film *Crouching Tiger, Hidden Dragon*.

## Staccato Beans
### from *Eight Memories in Watercolor*, Op. 1, No. 2
From the composer: "*Eight Memories in Watercolor* was written [in 1978–79] when I left Hunan to study at the Central Conservatory of Music in Beijing. It was my Opus One. The Cultural Revolution had just ended, China just opened its doors, I was immersed in studying Western classical and modern music, but I was also homesick. I longed for the folksongs and savored the memories of my childhood. Therefore, I wrote my first piano work as a diary of longing."

*Practice and Performance Tips*
- This happy music needs absolutely clarity throughout in touch and rhythm.
- The composer has created exquisite detail in articulation.
- Practice hands separately at a slow tempo, observing carefully articulations and dynamics.
- In the left hand in measures 13–18 the top voice is not tied, it is a slur to a *staccato* note.
- Move to practicing hands together, retaining all articulations and dynamics, and keeping a steady tempo throughout.
- Though the piece has driving rhythm, make certain that your playing is not tense, but instead has bubbly excitement, with a buoyant touch.
- As you increase your practice tempo, do not rush! Maintain steadiness no matter what your practice tempo.
- The composer invites the player to play the repeat faster. With this in mind, contain the tempo the first time.
- Use absolutely no sustaining pedal in this music.

## PYOTR IL'YICH TCHAIKOVSKY
(1840–1893, Russian)

Tchaikovsky was the great Russian composer of the nineteenth century who achieved the most international success, and whose symphonies, ballets, operas, chamber music and piano music continue to be a central part of the repertoire. Of his piano works, *The Seasons*, Op. 37bis, *Album for the Young*, Op. 39 and his concerto are most familiar to present day pianists and teachers. *Album for the Young* was written in four days in May of 1878, with revisions later that year before publication in October. It was during this year that Tchaikovsky left his teaching post at the St. Petersburg Conservatory and began composing and conducting full time, a move made financially possible by the patronage of Nadezhda von Meck.

## The Organ Grinder Sings
### from *Album for the Young*, Op. 39, No. 24
Much of *Album for the Young* is inspired by folksongs, capturing observations and experiences from childhood in 24 fanciful miniatures. Tchaikovsky heard the tune in "The Organ Grinder" when traveling in Italy.

*Practice and Performance Tips*
- Since this piece is really about the prominent melody, it is recommended that you get to know the tune very well first, playing only the top note of the right hand.
- If you play this over and over until you know it well, it will help to train your ear as to the priorities when you add the rest of the piece, which is the melody's accompaniment.
- Practice the left hand alone throughout.
- Practice the right hand alone, adding the rest to the melody.
- Notice that Tchaikovsky has given detailed articulation to the melody in the right hand, but has not marked any articulation in the left hand for measures 1–12. Practice a gentle, steady accompaniment in the left hand here.
- The biggest challenge begins in measure 16, when the music becomes busier, but must remain quiet.
- The *marcato* marking in measure 16 is for the right-hand melody only.
- Tchaikovsky challenges further by keeping the same motion but asking for **pp** in measure 24.
- From measure 16 to the end, the top note melody must predominate. The rest should be a murmuring accompaniment, and not sound frantic.

— Richard Walters, editor

*These pieces were previously published in the following*
*Schirmer Performance Editions volumes.*

Invention No. 8 in F Major, BWV 779
**from *J.S. Bach: Two-Part Inventions***
**edited by Christopher Taylor**

Bach: Prelude in D Major, BWV 936
**from *J.S. Bach: Nineteen Little Preludes***
**edited by Christos Tsitsaros**

Barber: Poison Ivy from *Fresh from West Chester (Some Jazzings)*
Bartók: Joc cu bâta (Stick Dance) from *Roumanian Folk Dances*
Dello Joio: Bright from *Suite for Piano*
Muczynski: Morning Promenade from *A Summer Journal,* Op. 19, No. 1
Shostakovich: Lyrical Waltz from *Dances of the Dolls*
Tan Dun: Staccato Beans from *Eight Memories in Watercolor,* Op. 1, No. 2
**from *The 20th Century: Upper Intermediate Level***
**edited by Richard Walters**

Bagatelle in A minor ("Für Elise"), WoO 59
**from *Beethoven: Für Elise and Other Bagatelles***
**edited by Matthew Edwards**

Prelude in D-flat Major ("Raindrop"), Op. 28, No. 15
**from *Chopin: Preludes***
**edited by Brian Ganz**

La fille aux cheveux de lin
**from *Debussy: Seven Favorite Pieces***
**edited by Christopher Harding**

Nottorno
**from *Grieg: Selected Lyric Pieces***
**edited by William Westney**

# The Organ Grinder Sings

from *Album for the Young*

Pyotr Il'yich Tchaikovsky
Op. 39, No. 24

Тихо [Calm] (♩ = 120-130)

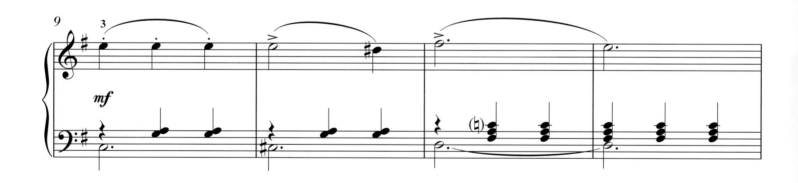

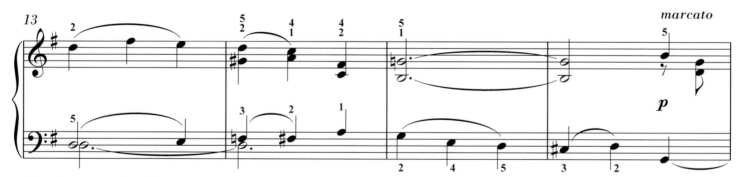

*marcato*

Fingerings are editorial suggestions.

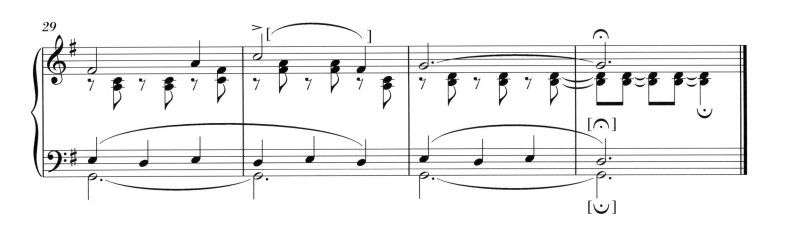

# March of the Grasshoppers

from *Music for Children*

Sergei Prokofiev
Op. 65, No. 7

Fingerings are editorial suggestions.

**Poco meno mosso**

# Prelude in D Major

Johann Sebastian Bach
BWV 936

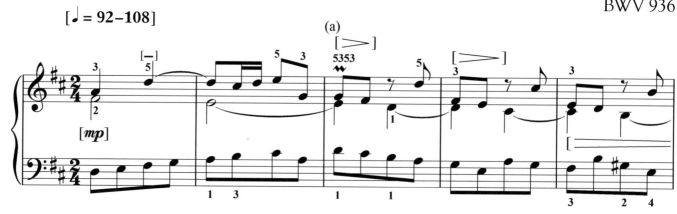

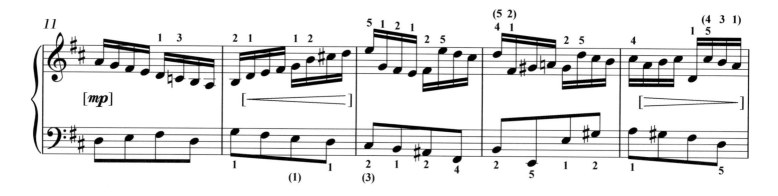

(a)

Fingerings are editorial suggestions.

# Invention No. 8 in F Major

Johann Sebastian Bach
BWV 779

Fingerings are editorial suggestions.

# Bagatelle in A Minor
## ("Für Elise")

Ludwig van Beethoven
WoO 59

**Poco moto**

*Traditionally played as D; E in the manuscript and first edition.
Fingerings are editorial suggestions.

*See footnote on p. 12.

*See footnote on p. 12.
**Some editions have:

*See footnote on p. 12.

**Alternately:

# War Dance

from *30 Pieces for Children*

Dmitri Kabalevsky
Op. 27, No. 19

**Allegro energico [♩ = c. 146]**

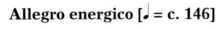

Fingerings are editorial suggestions.

# Lyrical Waltz
## from *Dances of the Dolls*

Dmitri Shostakovich

Fingerings are editorial suggestions.

# Träumerei
### (Reverie)
from *Scenes from Childhood (Kinderszenen)*

Robert Schumann
Op. 15, No. 7

*pedal with discretion
Fingerings are editorial suggestions.

# La fille aux cheveux de lin

from *Préludes*, Book 1

Claude Debussy
L. 117, No. 8

**Très calme et doucement expressif** [♩ = 66]

Fingerings are by the composer.

# Etude
## from *Children's Album*, Book 1

Aram Khachaturian

**Allegro moderato**

Fingerings are editorial suggestions.

# Song Without Words in F-sharp minor

("Venetian Gondola Song")

from *Songs Without Words*

Felix Mendelssohn
Op. 30, No. 6

**Allegretto tranquillo**

Fingerings are editorial suggestions.

# Etude in A Major
## from *30 Pieces for Children*

Dmitri Kabalevsky
Op. 27, No. 26

Fingerings are editorial suggestions.

# Tarantella
from *Music for Children*

Sergei Prokofiev
Op. 65, No. 4

Fingerings are editorial suggestions.

*to Gloria*

# Morning Promenade

from *A Summer Journal*

Robert Muczynski
Op. 19, No. 1

Fingerings are editorial suggestions.

# Notturno
## from *Lyric Pieces*

Edvard Grieg
Op. 54, No. 4

Fingerings are editorial suggestions.

# Bright
from *Suite for Piano*

Norman Dello Joio

Fingerings are editorial suggestions.

Copyright, 1945, by G. Schirmer, Inc.
International Copyright Secured

# Prelude in D-flat Major
## ("Raindrop")

Frédéric Chopin
Op. 28, No. 15

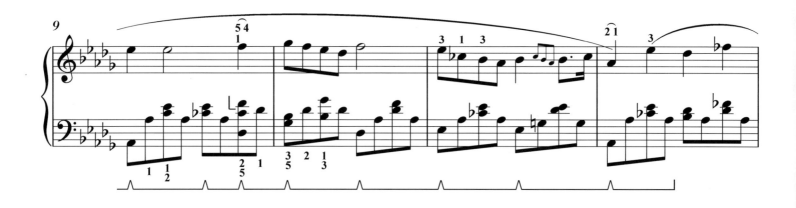

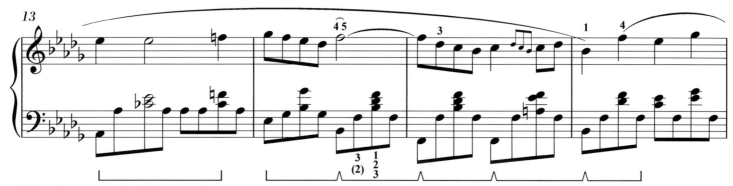

Fingerings are editorial suggestions.

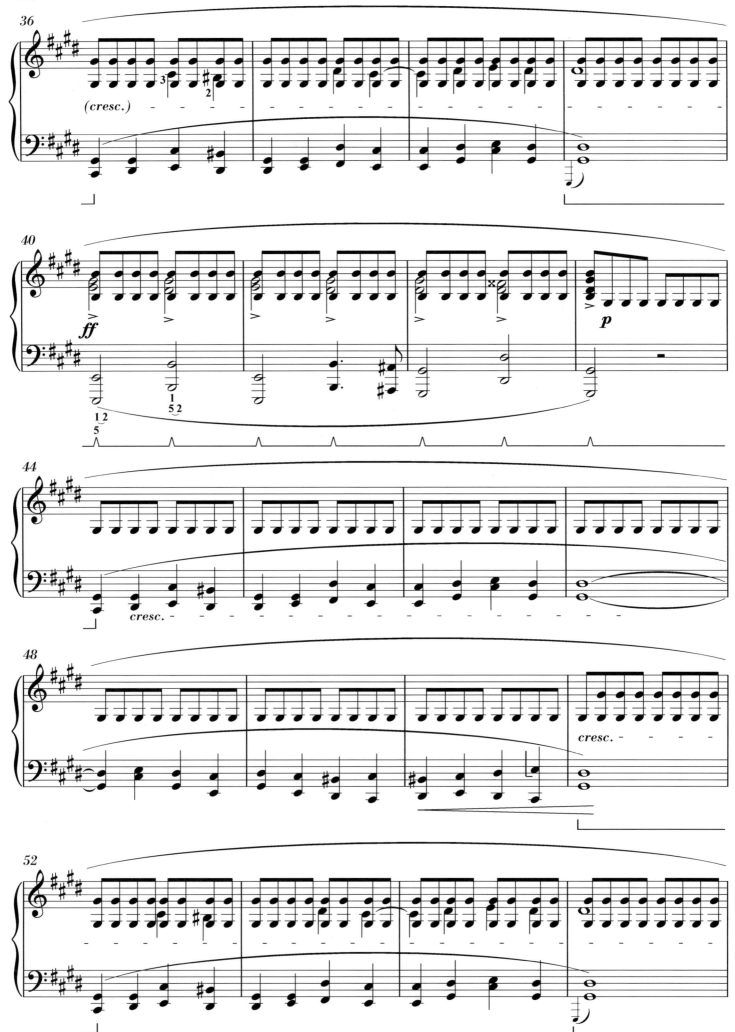

# Joc cu bâta
## (Stick Dance)
### from *Roumanian Folk Dances*

Béla Bartók

Fingerings are by the composer.

# Poison Ivy

from *Fresh from West Chester (Some Jazzings)*

Samuel Barber

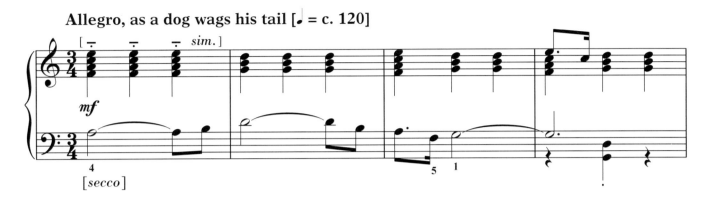

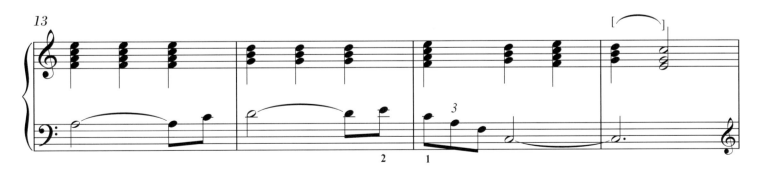

On the cover of the manuscript Barber wrote: "A country-dance that isn't. Accredited to, and blamed on T.T. Garboriasky—July 1925."
Fingerings are editorial suggestions.

# Toccata
## from Sonata No. 6 in A Major

Pietro Domenico Paradies [Paradisi]

Fingerings, tempo, and dynamics are editorial suggestions.
Play eighth notes, in right or left hand, slightly detached throughout.

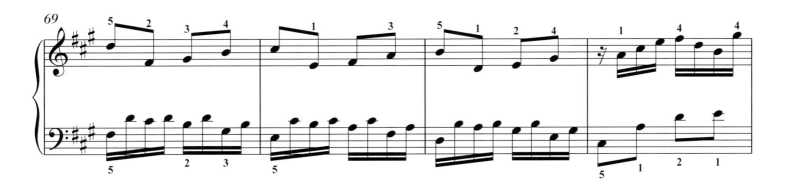

# Staccato Beans

from *Eight Memories in Watercolor*

Tan Dun
Op. 1, No. 2

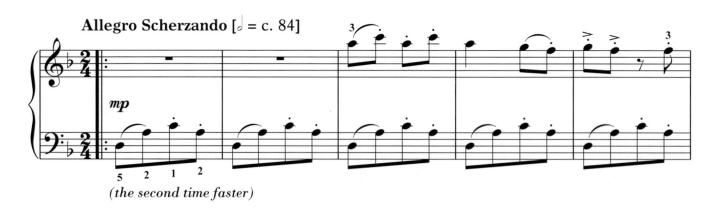

*(the second time faster)*

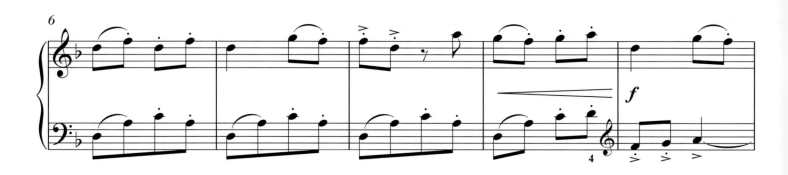

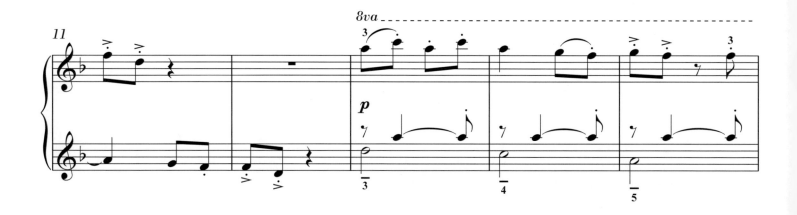

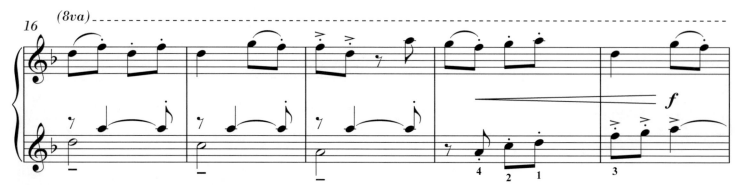

Fingerings are editorial suggestions.